Our WILD™ WORLD SERIES

Alligators and Crocodiles

NorthWord Press
Chanhassen, Minnesota

DEDICATION
For Sherry and Cliff and *Melanerpes erythrocephalus*
—D.D.

© NorthWord Press, 2003

Photography © 2003: Brian Kenney: cover, pp. 18, 34, 36-37; Tom & Therisa Stack/Tom Stack & Associates: p. 4; Doug Perrine/Seapics.com: pp. 5, 22; Michael H. Francis: p. 7; Gary Milburn/Tom Stack & Associates: p. 8; Mike Parry/Tom Stack & Associates: pp. 10, 27, 28; Rose Isaacs/Seapics.com: pp. 12-13; Wayne Lynch: pp. 14, 31, 39, 42, 44; Gary Kramer/garykramer.net: pp. 17, 38; Saul Gonor/Seapics.com: pp. 20-21; Masa Ushioda/Seapics.com: pp. 24-25; Carlos Navarro/Seapics.com: back cover, p. 33; Allen Blake Sheldon: pp. 40-41.

Illustrations by Jennifer Owings Dewey
Designed by Russell S. Kuepper
Edited by Judy Gitenstein
Cover image: American alligator (*Alligator mississippiensis*)

NorthWord Press
18705 Lake Drive East
Chanhassen, MN 55317
1-800-328-3895
www.northwordpress.com

Library of Congress Cataloging-in-Publication Data

Dennard, Deborah.
    Alligators and crocodiles / Deborah Dennard ; illustrations by Jennifer Owings Dewey.
        p. cm. – (Our wild world series)
    Summary: Describes the physical characteristics and behavior of various species of alligators and crocodiles from around the world.
    ISBN 1-55971-860-9 (hardcover) – ISBN 1-55971-859-5 (softcover)
    1. Alligators—Juvenile literature. 2. Crocodiles—Juvenile literature. [1. Alligators. 2. Crocodiles. I. Dewey, Jennifer, ill. II. Title. III. Series.

QL666.C925 D46 2003
597.98—dc21
                                                            2002043117

Printed in Malaysia

10 9 8 7 6 5 4 3 2 1

Our WILD™ WORLD
SERIES

Alligators and Crocodiles

Deborah Dennard
Illustrations by Jennifer Owings Dewey

NORTHWORD PRESS
Chanhassen, Minnesota

ALLIGATORS and crocodiles have been around since the time of the dinosaurs. In ancient times they looked very much like alligators and crocodiles do today. Even with their long history, these amazing creatures remain a mystery to people.

Alligators and crocodiles are reptiles, like snakes, lizards, and turtles. All reptiles have dry, scaly skin. Alligators and crocodiles have special scales. They are like suits of armor, with thick, tough plates that protect them.

Crocs open their mouths to display and to help cool off their bodies when they get too warm.

American alligators are found in shallow pools of fresh water through much of the southern part of the United States.

5

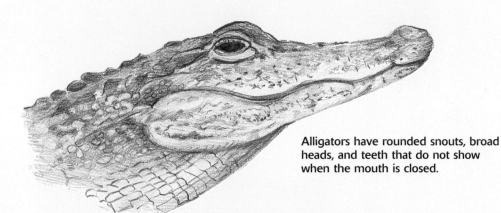

Alligators have rounded snouts, broad heads, and teeth that do not show when the mouth is closed.

Crocodiles have pointed snouts, narrower heads and teeth that do show when the mouth is closed.

Alligators, crocodiles, and all other reptiles are cold-blooded. This means that their body temperature is the same as the air or water around them. Reptiles control their body temperature by sitting in the sun to get warm or by sitting in the shade or the water to cool off. Alligators and crocodiles sometimes sit in the sun with their mouths held open. This probably helps them to cool their heads as they warm their bodies.

Alligators and crocodiles are very

The very rare American crocodile is found only in
extreme southern Florida and some islands in the Caribbean.

similar, but there are some differences. Alligators have a rounded mouth and snout, or nose, and a broad head. Crocodiles have a triangular-shaped head and a pointy snout and mouth. Some crocodiles have a large tooth in the bottom jaw near the front that can be seen when their mouths are closed. On other crocodiles, many teeth show. Alligators do not show their teeeth when their mouths are closed. Crocodile eyes are a bit smaller and closer together than alligator eyes. This makes crocodiles appear to be cross-eyed.

Black caimans are related to alligators and live in Central and South America.
They are prized for their fine black hides.

There are only about 23 different kinds, or species (SPEE-sees), of alligators and crocodiles in the world. Ten of these are alligators or caimans (CAY-muns), which are very similar. Thirteen of these species are crocodiles. As a group scientists call them all crocodilians (croc-uh-DILL-ee-uns). Sometimes they call them crocs for short.

Most crocodilians cannot survive in extreme temperatures. Most do not live in places where the temperature freezes. They do not live where the weather is too hot and dry. Crocodilians dig down into the ground for protection (pro-TEK-shun) from heat and drought (DROWT). A drought is a long stretch of time without rain. Crocs dig shallow holes where water and mud collect, called mud wallows or gator holes. Mud and water may stay in these gator holes long after other areas are dry. The mud and water help to keep crocodilians from overheating.

Crocodilian
FUNFACT:

Crocodilian hearts beat as slowly as 5 beats per minute in cool water, 50 degrees Fahrenheit (10 Celsius). They beat as quickly as 45 beats per minute in warm water, 82 degrees Fahrenheit (28 Celsius).

This Australian saltwater crocodile was found swimming in the ocean at the Great Barrier Reef.

Water is important to all crocodilians. They live in or near rivers, lakes, streams, ponds, pools, marshes, and swamps. The saltwater crocodile from Australia lives in salt water in the ocean, both near shore and in open waters.

Alligators and crocodiles spend most of their lives in the water. Their flat tails act as powerful flippers. Their tails steer them through the water quickly and quietly by swishing back and forth in a pattern that looks like the letter "S." Crocodilians' feet are held next to the body when they swim. Their feet paddle slowly to tread water when they float.

When a crocodilian treads water, only its eyes and nostrils are visible. The rest of its body is hidden just below the surface. With its nostrils just above the water a crocodilian can breathe air. With its eyes just peeking above the water it can watch for danger and dinner.

Crocodilians grow new teeth throughout their lives. As the old teeth break or become dull, they fall out and are replaced by new teeth. Crocodilians can have hundreds, even thousands, of teeth in their lifetime.

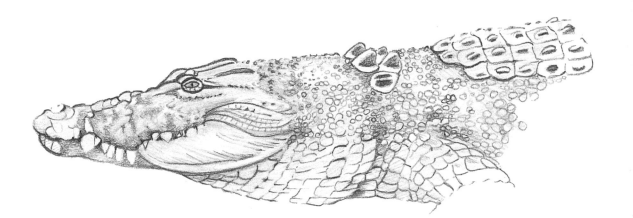

Crocodilians have different scales on different parts of their bodies.
Some are thick and spiky for protection.
Others are smaller and thinner for easier movement.

Alligators and crocodiles have scales of all different shapes and sizes on their bodies. The scaly skin on the head is very strong and tight and made of different shapes, like a quilt. The scales on the back are very hard and usually have a raised ridge for protection. Scales on the legs are shaped like diamonds or circles. Scales on the belly are nearly square.

Each type of scale is specially suited to each part of the body. For example, the square belly scales are large and smooth and make it easy to drag their bellies across the ground. The hard, ridged back scales give excellent protection. The small, circular scales on the legs are flexible for moving.

Alligators and crocodiles do not have lips. They cannot keep water out of their mouths. Instead, their wind pipes close up. Even their ears and nostrils shut down when they are underwater.

Crocodilians' eyes are protected from the water by an extra set of eyelids, which are so thin that crocs can see through them. These eyelids do not move up and down. They move from side to side across the eyes. Crocs automatically (ah-toe-MAT-ik-lee) cover their eyes with these extra eyelids when underwater. The eyelids work like swimming goggles and help them to see underwater.

Crocodilian
FUNFACT:

Alligators and crocodiles store fat in their bodies and can live as long as 1 or 2 years without eating.

When underwater, crocodilian eyes are protected by extra, see-through eyelids.

This caiman can move rapidly on land or swim swiftly in the water.

Alligators and crocodiles can hold their breath underwater for as long as 6 hours. They can do this because of the special way their hearts are built. Their hearts are divided into 4 parts, or chambers. All other reptiles have hearts with only 3 chambers. Alligators and crocodiles sit very still underwater and live with very little oxygen (AWK-zih-jin). Even when they are above water, they breathe very slowly, as little as 3 breaths per minute. People breathe about 18 times per minute at rest and more when in motion.

In water and on land, crocodilians are able to move very well. Their back feet are webbed. This helps them in swimming. Their legs and hips are flexible and jointed to help them move in many different ways. All of their muscles are very powerful.

One scientist has named 24 different ways alligators and crocodiles can move. They can walk on the bottom of a lake or river, or float and paddle at the top of the water. They can float upright in the water with only their heads held above water. They can walk in many ways on land, from dragging their bodies slowly to galloping quickly like a horse.

Crocodilian
FUNFACT:

Crocs have been seen running or galloping on land as fast as 26 miles (42 kilometers) per hour for short sprints.

Alligators and crocodiles are carnivores (KAR-nuh-vorz). That means they eat meat. They get their food by hunting and killing other animals, or prey (PRAY). Crocodilians are excellent hunters. Babies and small crocs eat animals as small as snails, insects, worms, and shrimp. The larger the croc, the larger the animal it can eat.

Alligators and crocodiles with very narrow snouts eat mostly fish. Their small snouts make it easier to move in the water but harder to catch food on land. These crocs usually have needle-like teeth for catching and holding fish.

Alligators and crocodiles with wider snouts can eat larger animals and a greater variety of animals that live on land or in the water.

Most crocodilians lie in the water to wait for their prey. A croc's prey is usually caught when the prey stops to take a drink of water and does not see the hungry hunter waiting. When its prey comes close enough, a croc can move quickly. It can even jump in the air or lunge out of the water onto land. A croc will usually grab its prey and drag it underwater.

Crocodilian
FUNFACT:

The largest of all crocodilians are the saltwater crocodiles from Australia. When fully grown, they can kill water buffalo and horses.

American alligators lie in wait for their prey in shallow water.

A raccoon drinking at the water's edge has become the prey of an alligator hiding in the water.

Some crocodilians have special diets. The common caiman in South America can feed on piranha (pih-RAH-nah) fish. The sharp teeth of the piranha are not able to bite through the caimans' tough scales.

Some crocs have special ways of hunting for their prey. The African slender-snouted crocodile uses its tail to gather fish in shallow water. Then it sweeps up the fish in its jaws.

All alligators and crocodiles swallow small animals whole. Larger prey animals may take days to consume. Saltwater crocodiles push the body of a large animal such as a water buffalo up under a ledge or rock in the water. They return for many days to feast.

Nile crocodiles change their diet as they grow. Babies up to 20 inches (50 centimeters) long eat insects. Small adults up to 10 feet (3 meters) eat fish and birds. Large adults up to 16 feet (5 meters) eat large animals, like zebras.

Nile crocodiles in Africa and saltwater crocodiles in Australia may attack people who come too close to the water. That is why people must be careful when visiting the places where these wild and dangerous animals live.

Crocodilians eat stones that stay in their stomachs. Scientists believe these stones do 2 jobs. Crocs use their sharp teeth to kill prey, not to chew them into little pieces. The stones help to crush the food once it is in their stomachs. Acids in their stomachs also work to digest the food.

The weight of the swallowed stones also helps crocodilians to float just below the surface of the water. This is the same reason human divers wear weight belts. The extra weight helps keep their bodies below the water's surface.

Crocodilian
FUNFACT:

Adult crocs can eat as much as 20 percent, or one-fifth, of their total body weight in a meal. This would be like a 100-pound (45-kilogram) person eating 20 pounds (9 kilograms) of food at once!

The senses of sight, hearing, and smell are very important to alligators and crocodiles. Crocs can see in color. They can see near and far, and they can see at night and during the day. The pupils of their eyes are larger at night to allow in more light. Their pupils are smaller and slit-like during the day to keep out too much light. Their good vision helps them search for food.

Underwater, crocs cannot hear very well because their ears are closed to keep out water. Above the water they can hear the bellows, roars, moans, grunts, and other sounds that other adult crocs make. They also can hear the high-pitched sounds made by their babies. It is important for alligators and crocodiles to hear well because they are the noisiest of all of the reptiles. They use sounds to communicate.

Scientists have learned that crocodilians can sense very small vibrations (vie-BRAY-shuns) in the water with the bumps on their faces and mouths. These bumps feel the movement of even a tiny ripple in the water. They are very helpful in finding food.

The Australian freshwater crocodile is much smaller and less aggressive than the Australian saltwater crocodile.

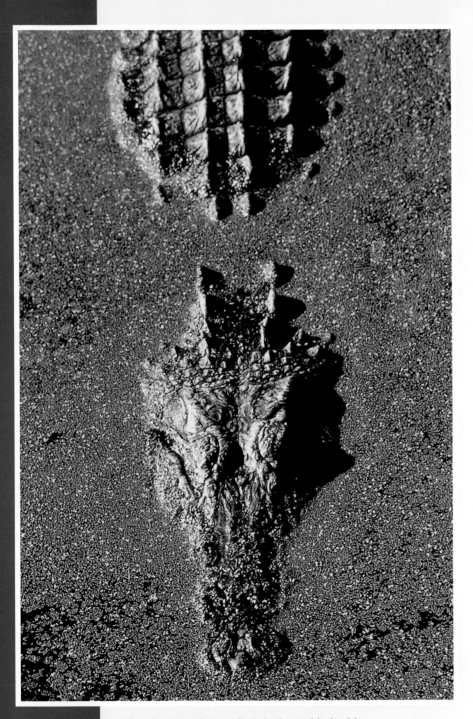

Alligator and crocodile nostrils are located on the top of the very end of their long snouts. This allows them to breathe when most of their bodies are underwater. Crocodilians also use their nostrils for their sense of smell. Scientists think crocs can recognize others by smell. Babies may even be able to smell adult males nearby. This may help them to get away safely. This is important because adult crocs sometimes eat baby crocs.

A crocodilian lying perfectly still on the bank of a river or floating in the water can look just like a log. Even their rough, scaly skin looks like the bark of a tree. This gives them very good camouflage (KAM-uh-flaj). Camouflage allows an animal to hide by blending into the surrounding water, plants, dirt, or rocks.

Tiny floating plants called duckweed help this American alligator to hide in a pool of water.

Crocodilians have very few predators (PRED-uh-torz), or animals that hunt them for food, in the wild. This is because they are so large and are very alert.

There are some dangers, though. Larger alligators and crocodiles may eat smaller ones. In South America, jaguars (JAG-wahrs) may attack crocodilian nests. Anacondas (an-uh-CON-duhs), the largest snakes in the world, may eat smaller caimans. In Australia, large lizards dig into crocodile nests to eat the eggs. In Africa, hippos, lions, and elephants have been known to kill Nile crocodiles. This is unusual and happens only if the predators are frightened or if the crocodiles threaten their babies.

Fully-grown adults sometimes may fight with each other until one of them dies. A fight to the death can happen when an alligator or crocodile is protecting its territory or home. It also can happen when a female is protecting her nest. Some scientists think that adult crocs protect nests of babies so they can eat the babies themselves. Crocs sometimes fight during mating season. They also may fight among themselves during the dry season, when water and food become scarce.

Crocodilians in the wild may live to be 40 or 50 years old. Some scientists believe that a few individuals may live much longer, as long as 70 or 80 years.

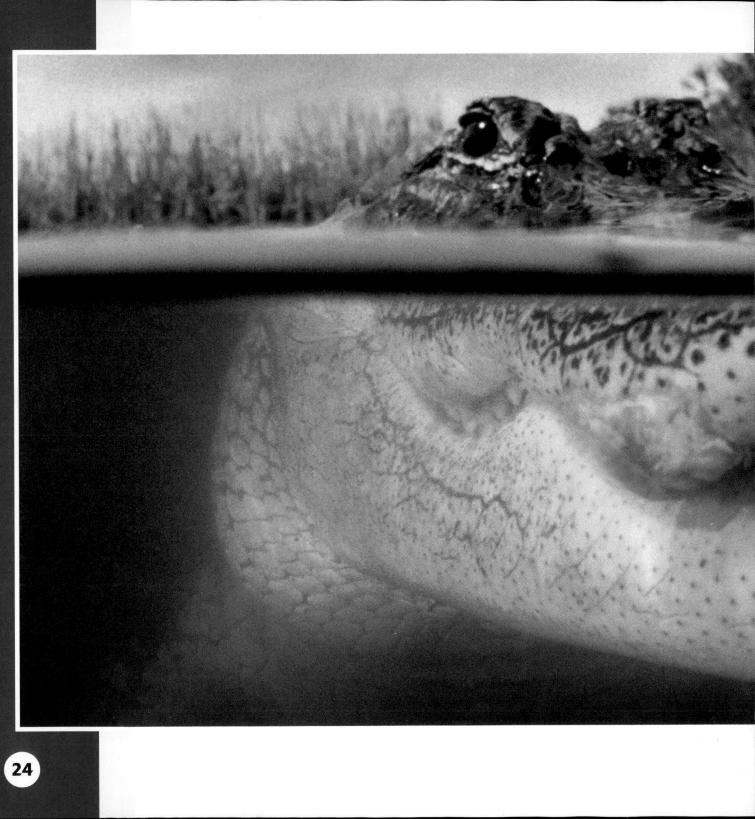

Crocs cannot fully close their mouths underwater. To keep from swallowing water, their wind pipes close when underwater.

Most crocodilian mothers give their babies some protection. Mother Nile crocodiles lead their babies around for nearly 2 years, and the youngsters obediently follow. Scientists do not believe that the mothers teach their babies anything during this time. The babies follow from instinct and are protected from danger just because their large mother is near.

Sure signs of the mating season for alligators and crocodiles are the loud noises they make. Males and females make a sound that is a lot like the roar of a lion. They use the sounds to find each other for mating. They also communicate by slapping their heads on the water or thrashing their tails in the water. With noises, crocs announce their home territories and their interest in finding a mate.

Crocodilian
FUNFACT:

Australians call saltwater crocodiles "salties" for short. They call freshwater crocodiles "freshies" for short.

Saltwater crocodiles strike with great speed and strength.
They may grab their prey and thrash around with it underwater until it is dead.

These saltwater crocodile hatchlings are leaving their eggs and their nest for the first time. Most will not survive to be 19-foot giants.

Usually the female builds the nest for her babies. Some species of alligators and crocodiles build large nests. Others build smaller nests. Some dig holes to use as nests. Some build mounds as nests. Some nests are a combination of holes and mounds.

Schneider's dwarf caimans in South America have very unusual nests. They often dig holes around the base of a large termite mound and lay their eggs there. This helps to keep the eggs warm.

American crocodiles dig a hole for a nest in a spot above the high water mark, so that the nest does not become flooded. American alligators build large mud, stick, and leaf nests above ground. These nests are so large and have been built for so many thousands of years that they have changed the land where alligators live, building up soil above water level. That is why alligators are sometimes called living bulldozers.

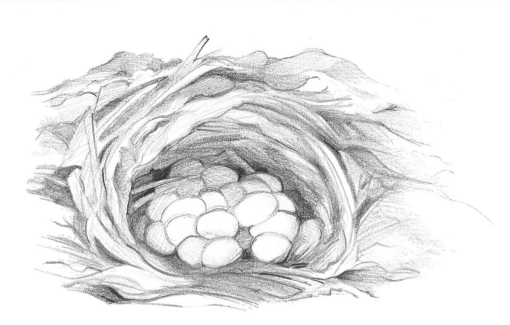

These American alligator eggs will stay warm because the decaying plants in the nest create heat.

Scientists have spent a lot of time studying the way in which American alligators build their nests. First the alligators make a path through the brush to find the right place for their nest. The nest may be 7 feet (2.1 meters) wide. It may be 42 inches (about 1 meter) high.

The nest is made of twigs, leaves, sticks, and dirt carried by the mother alligator into the nest. Females build their nests during the night and then dig a hole in the nest. There they lay their eggs. Using their back feet they carefully place each egg safely down in the nesting hole.

Baby crocs use a bump at the end of their snouts called
an egg tooth to make their way out of their eggs.

Once the eggs are laid, the mother alligator covers them over with more leaves and sticks. She stays near the nest until the babies hatch. Her presence may help to keep the babies safe. As the leaves and dirt rot, they create heat and keep the eggs warm.

After 2 or 3 months, the eggs are ready to hatch. The babies make a little croaking sound from inside the egg that easily can be heard outside of the nest. They begin to make their way out of their eggs using a bump on the end of their noses called an egg tooth. The mother may sit by and let the babies hatch themselves. She also may open the nest with her strong jaws and sharp teeth, and gently help the babies out of their eggs. The mother even may carry the babies to the water in her mouth.

A group of baby alligators is called a pod.

The mother alligator stays near the babies for a while to protect them. Sometimes they even sit on her back. When they first hatch, the babies are about 8.5 inches (21.6 centimeters) long. By the time they are just 1 year old, they will be 24 inches (61 centimeters) long. Still, many babies are lost in the first year. Animals such as herons, snakes, wildcats, otters, turtles, skunks, raccoons, large catfish, and even other alligators may eat the babies.

Those that survive will grow to be somewhere between 6 and 12 feet (1.8 to 3.7 meters) long. There have been rare examples of extra large alligators. The largest American alligator ever measured was found in 1890. It was about 19 feet (5.8 meters) long. Alligators this large are very, very unusual.

In addition to the American alligator, there is one other main species of alligator. This is the Chinese alligator. The Chinese alligator is a rare animal found mostly around the Yangtze (YANG-see) River. Chinese alligators grow to about 6.6 feet (2 meters) long. Chinese alligators are unusual because they can live where temperatures may freeze. The only other crocodilian that can stand freezing temperatures is the American alligator.

To survive the cold, Chinese alligators dig burrows between 5 feet (1.5 meters) and 60 feet (18 meters) long. There they slow down their heartbeats and their breathing and wait until the weather becomes warmer. They may be inactive for 6 or 7 months of every year.

Crocodilian
FUNFACT:

Chinese alligators may float in icy cold water or just below a layer of ice. As long as their nostrils are above the ice for breathing, they can survive.

This baby caiman shows the bony eyebrow ridges that make this croc appear to be wearing glasses.

Caimans are so closely related to alligators they are like first cousins. Their heads are not as broad as an alligator's head and not as narrow as the heads of crocodiles. Their belly scales are harder and tougher than the belly scales of any other croc in the world. For many years this made them safe from hunters because their skins were too hard to tan into leather. New ways have been found to soften their hides though, so now they also are hunted for their skins.

Caimans live in Central and South America. They get their food by drowning and crushing their prey. Then they stick their heads straight up out of the water to swallow with a gulp.

They use their back legs and feet differently than any other alligator or crocodile. Like a dog, they rub their eyes and scratch themselves with their back legs. They even hold on to food with their back legs as they tear it into pieces with their powerful jaws.

Caimans are like alligators because of the shape of their rounded snout and their teeth, which are hidden when their mouths are closed. Most caimans are smaller than alligators.

There are 8 species of caimans. The smallest is the dwarf caiman that lives around the Amazon and Orinoco Rivers in South America. It grows to be only about 5 feet (1.5 meters) long. In fact, this is the smallest of any alligator or crocodile in the world.

The largest of all of the caimans is the black caiman that lives in quiet rivers and grassy wetlands in Peru, Ecuador, and Colombia. It grows to be 19.7 feet (6 meters) long.

The beautiful color of the black caiman's skin is the main reason it is an endangered (en-DANE-jurd) animal. It is a rich, dark shade of black. Hunters kill these animals to sell their skins. The skins are made into purses, boots, shoes, and wallets. Even though there are laws to protect the black caimans, many are still killed illegally. Without the protection of people, they may become extinct (ex-TINKD). This would mean that there would be none left in the world.

Common caimans are not endangered. There may be as many as 4 million in Venezuela. There are enough caimans in Venezuela to allow some hunting.

Crocodilian
FUNFACT:

Another name for the common caiman is the spectacled caiman. Bony ridges around the eyes make them look like they are wearing glasses, or spectacles.

The American crocodile lives from the very tip of the state of Florida down into Central and South America and even on a few Caribbean Islands.

American crocodiles like to live in brackish water, or water that is slightly salty. Brackish water is found where the fresh water of lakes and rivers meets the salt water of oceans. These places are called estuaries (ESS-chew-air-eez).

American crocodiles eat mostly fish and grow to be about 13 feet (4 meters) long. People seldom see them because they are shy and move only at night. They also are very rare. About 10 years ago scientists estimated that no more than 500 American crocodiles were alive in Florida.

American crocodiles have learned to adapt to change. South of Miami, Florida, a colony, or group, of these crocs moved into manmade water canals built outside a power plant. The crocodiles build nests on dams made by people to hold water. Workers have seen female American crocodiles take mouthfuls of sand from a construction site to carry to their nests.

Temperature is important to these baby American crocodiles before they hatch. The eggs hatch males if the temperature of the nest is warm. The eggs hatch females if the nest is cooler.

Nile crocodiles are some of the most dangerous
animals in all of Africa.

In Africa, Nile crocodiles are strong and fierce hunters that grow to be 16.4 feet (5 meters) long. They can be found in large numbers in lakes and rivers. They eat fish. They also lie in wait for large mammals to come and drink the water. Nile crocodiles can kill animals as large as antelope, giraffes, zebras, lions, young hippos, and buffalo. They also eat carrion (KARE-ee-un), or animals that are already dead. Sometimes they gather in groups of over 100 to gorge themselves on carrion.

These fierce crocs are also dangerous to people. Records show that Nile crocodiles kill more people every year than all of the other dangerous animals in Africa combined.

This saltwater crocodile shows only the large bottom tooth. Other crocodile species show many teeth.

Australian saltwater crocodiles are the largest of all crocodilians. They can grow to be 19.7 feet (6 meters) long. They can weigh as much as 2,420 pounds (1,089 kilograms). The name can be confusing, though, because these crocodiles can be found in all types of water, not just salt water. They can be found in fresh water, brackish water, and salt water. They even can be found in the open oceans and have been tracked traveling as far as 688 miles (1,100 kilometers) through ocean waters.

As saltwater crocodiles grow, their diet changes. Until they are about 6.5 feet (2 meters) long, saltwater crocodiles eat fish, crabs, and turtles. Once they are bigger they hunt for larger fish, snakes, large water birds such as herons, and dingoes, which are Australian wild dogs. The largest of the saltwater crocs can attack and eat kangaroos, horses, wild pigs, and even water buffalo.

Freshwater crocodiles are found in the northern parts of Australia in rivers, streams, and ponds called billabongs. At just 6.5 feet (2 meters) long, freshwater crocodiles are much smaller than salt-water crocodiles and do not harm people. When they are young, they eat small animals, such as fish, insects, and spiders. As they grow they catch and eat water birds, lizards, and even wallabies, which are related to kangaroos.

Many of the native Australian people, or Aborigines (ab-uh-RIJ-uh-nees), believe that crocodiles are sacred animals. One belief is that all of Australia began as a crocodile. Another belief is that people owe their lives to a spirit called the Great Crocodile.

Crocodilian
FUNFACT:

Ancient Egyptians believed that Nile crocodiles were sacred, or holy. They even made thousands of crocodile mummies.

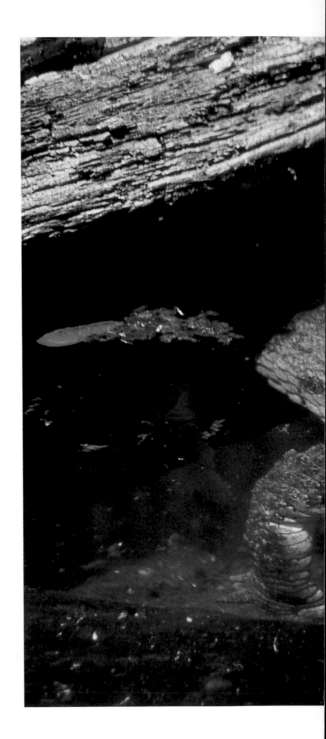

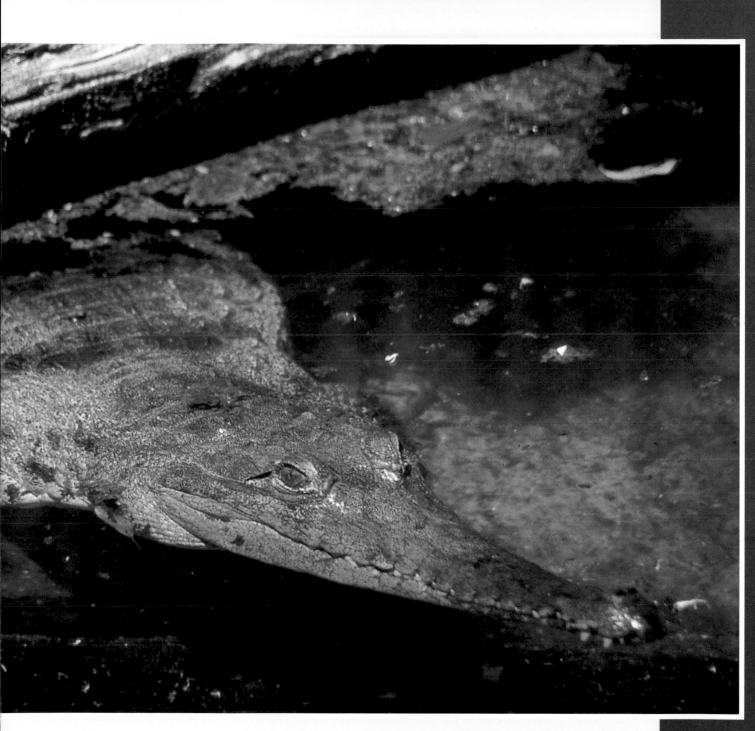

This grown freshwater crocodile now eats birds, snakes, lizards, and even wallabies.

Gharials have more than 100 teeth.

Gharials (GAR-ee-als), or gavials (GAV-ee-als), may be the most unusual of all crocodilians. Their legs are so small and weak that on land they are only able to slide their bodies slowly along. Unless they are warming themselves in the sun or laying their eggs, they stay in the water.

Gharials find their food in the water. They eat fish and frogs. They catch them by slashing their long, skinny, pointed snouts back and forth in the water. Their long snouts are well suited to catching prey in the water but not on land.

Gharials have more than 100 razor-sharp teeth. Males also have a large, ball-like bump on the end of their snouts. They live in rivers in the northern part of India and in Nepal, Pakistan, and Bangladesh. Some scientists think that gharials are a type of crocodile. Others think they are a completely different type of crocodilian and not a type of alligator or crocodile at all.

Alligators and crocodiles are strong and fierce hunters that are perfectly suited to the swamps, rivers, and waters where they live. They are some of the most specialized animals in the world. Much mystery surrounds these reptiles and much has yet to be learned. Crocodilians are ancient animals that managed to survive when the dinosaurs did not.

Crocodilian
FUNFACT:

Crocodilian fossils, ancient bones turned into rocks over time, show that these animals have not changed much since the time of the dinosaurs, about 65 million years ago.

This baby American alligator is too small to pose any threat to the turtle on which it sits. When it is full-grown, it could make a meal of the turtle.

In the past, many alligators and crocodiles were killed because people were afraid of them. Many more were killed to make belts and shoes and wallets from their skin. Yet today it may be their hides that help to save them. Many alligators and crocodiles are now raised on farms so their skins can be harvested. This helps crocs in the wild to survive. When people raise these reptiles for their skin and meat, they do not go into the wild to hunt them.

In most places it is against the law to hunt alligators and crocodiles. Laws have been passed to protect them.

Many of these animals are endangered because people have used their wet, swampy homes to make cities and farms. The areas where alligators and crocodiles live must remain swamps in order for these ancient reptiles to survive. People can help. Because of people, American alligators and Australian saltwater crocodiles are now thriving.

The more that scientists can learn about all crocodilians, the more people will be able to help them. With some work and caring, the world can be a place for people, alligators, and crocodiles, too.

Internet Sites

You can find out more interesting information about crocodiles, alligators, and lots of other wildlife by visiting these Internet sites.

http://animal.discovery.com/convergence/safari/crocs/croctour/croctour.html
Animal Planet.com

www.crocodilian.com — Crocodile Specialist Group

www.enchantedlearning.com — Enchanted Learning.com

www.flmnh.ufl.edu/natsci/herpetology/crocs/crocpics.htm
Florida Museum of Natural History

www.nationalgeographic.com/crocmap/ — National Geographic Society

www.pbs.org/wgbh/nova/crocs/ — Nova Online

www.oneworldmagazine.org/tales/crocs/index.html
One World Magazine

www.scz.org/animals/home.html — Sedgwick County Zoo

www.vanaqua.org/visitor_information/AquaFacts/crocodilians.htm
Vancouver Aquarium

Index

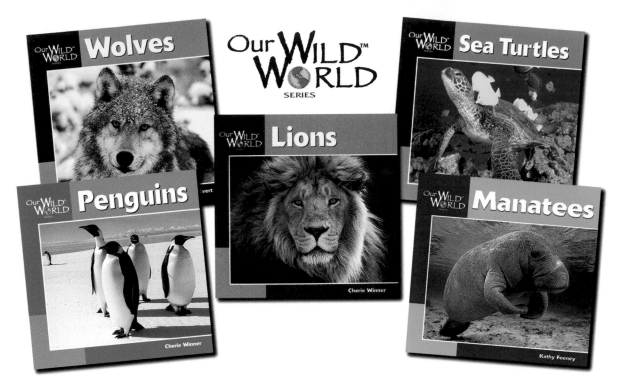

Titles available in the Our Wild World Series:

See your nearest bookseller, or order by phone 1-800-328-3895

NorthWord Press
Chanhassen, Minnesota